They Aren't Your Ducks

They Aren't Your Ducks

SALLY McGREEVEY HANNAY

RESOURCE *Publications* · Eugene, Oregon

THEY AREN'T YOUR DUCKS

Resource Publications
An Imprint of Wipf and Stock Publishers
199 W. 8th Ave., Suite 3
Eugene, OR 97401

www.wipfandstock.com

PAPERBACK ISBN: 978-1-7252-5752-8
HARDCOVER ISBN: 978-1-7252-5753-5
EBOOK ISBN: 978-1-7252-5754-2

Manufactured in the U.S.A.   02/28/20

For my ducks

Contents

THE RIVER NEVER WORRIES

Preface

MY FAMILY BIOLOGY

I have a son who is the equilibrium of the family.
He balances us like the ball on the seal's nose,
the keel of our boat, the lightning rod of our structure.
He carries us like a big square draft horse, rarely stumbling.
When he does stumble, we all taste a little dirt.

I have a son who is the memory of the family,
the scrapbook, the historian, storing snapshots
of unforgettable moments we have all forgotten.
He maps, safeguards and catalogs our journey.
When he isn't there to record our doings,
it is almost as if they didn't happen.

I have daughter who is the heart of us all,
the Geiger counter of our family soul.
She suffers all our losses
and notices all our improvements.
She finds our lost things, or weeps for them.
She is the tiger mother of us, as us.

My husband is the immune system,
the courage, the skin, the tough outer layer,
the defender against germs and intruders,
the maintainer and replacer of broken parts,
and the mechanic of our inner and outer workings.

I suppose I am the, sometimes hypersensitive, nervous system:
the worrier, the over-reactor, the panic button, the barking dog.

I surely need my daughter's heart,
and my son's balance—
my son's memory,
and my husband's courage.

I would be only nervous without them.

In the Great Big Middle

REPORTING A LOST CHILD

Yes, hello,
I'm not sure I've got the right number,
but I need to report a lost child
A Son
Twenty-five

I've tried before, but I don't think it was this number
It's been a while—
maybe years. . .

When he needs money

Yes, well, we thought so, but. . .
He went to a few meetings, so did I
My husband found him a good lawyer

Yes, I'll hold

Hello, yes about my son
Well—usually springtime
I understand. . .
I'm sure.
It's a busy time.

Are you, I mean, can you connect me with someone who can. . .?
Or are you the one who. . .?

We love him and just have to do something, right?
All kinds of mistakes, of course, just not knowing. . .
Or you could put me in touch with some others who. . .
I could call back.

I just want to be told what to do.

Yes, I can hold.

No, I'll keep holding.

SIMPLE

A full moon looking in my bathroom window
on a so quietly early winter morning.
Confident and lonely Mr. Moon, Saying:
"Oh dear, you are awake and watchful, again.
I am lighting your universe
and still
just
happy and round and
simple as a circle."

SALVATION ROAD

What stirs your fear?
The ironies?
The miracles?
When the warm, sunny evening
becomes an earthquake.
A child is singing in one room and
a good woman grieves a great loss in another.
Listening to the cold, howling wind
from a warm bed,
aching with unsettled, settling.

If you could name the sorrow storms like hurricanes
Betty
Candice
Donna
have experts checking the radar
specialists trained in knowing and naming and counting
whether there's one finger, or two, or a thousand on the trigger
professionals dedicated to listening
expectantly
for the first rumble
of sob bending sorrow
reliably predicting
the duration and estimating the
extent of damage—

Would recognizing the face,
and locating the coordinates,
be a comfort or a worry?

One day you are right on itinerary:
the trip tic is operational,
the GPS is singing your song.

Then, suddenly or slowly,
you are lost in "Route Recalculation"

Wandering the loop trail,
wailing the dead end
plodding, stubbornly, the slough of despair,
paying the toll,
waiting the jam,
sweating the detour,
missing the exit
one wrong lane and you're in a gang war. . ..
"This is not how it looks on the map!"

You can park and climb in the trunk.
Or, you can wad up the map,
jump in the back seat,
roll down the window,
sniff the air like a pup and
let the Driver drive.

BITCH KITTY

When I was learning the world from my mother, she would say,
"Now that's a Bitch Kitty,"
to describe thankless, female tasks like:
cooking Thanksgiving dinner for hordes of ungrateful relatives,
cleaning out the refrigerator, paying the bills—
any continuous, tedious, unrewarded efforts— Bitch Kitties.

She would also sometimes say, proudly, of one of her friends,
"Betty sure can be a Bitch Kitty," meaning,
Betty didn't tip a rude waiter, or told off a bad teacher;
Betty flipped off a reckless driver on the freeway:
any righteous, unladylike reaction earned the Bitch Kitty handle.

My Mom was a Bitch Kitty.
I wanted to be a Bitch Kitty when I grew up.
You wanted to be one,
so you wouldn't have to do one.

Over time and generations, Bitch Kitties have matured, weathered, seasoned,
and like art, developed an edge.

Some of those age-old triggers still and always make the Bitch Kitty tick.
The pimples, sties and stumbles of kitty husbands are always juicy catnip.

Hormones, holidays, traffic? Sure.
How about that sticky build-up of rude oblivious actions by rude oblivious
people? Absofuckenlutely.

(Insertion of the F word in the middle of adverbs and adjectives is also
symptomatic of the New Kitty Edge.)

I've known modern day Kitties who make their thankless boss's coffee with toilet water; (this still has the passive aggressive mark of the late model kitty, but you can see the edging).

I recently heard a Kitty turn down an insincere dinner invitation to shave her legs, and another send back a red pen edit of her mother-in-law's disingenuous Thank-You note.

I wonder: is this random and careless scratching and clawing?
Is just any furniture her scratching post?
I don't think so.

Is the Bitch Kitty a much maligned and righteous,
Indifuckinspensable,
Superhero-Warrior-Kitty?
Is she the functional howl;
the scratch at the door;
the "me-ow" as is "me-ouch;"
the clawer of convention for the:
"I love the new range hood, but I miss my soul," Kitty?

Is the Bitch Kitty a last defense against the trendy
Bonsai Kitty carefully stuffed into a bottle to stay
cute and silent and small like a clutch purse?

Is she the furry and veracious anecdote for:
"I'm nothing like my mother, but this is no fun at all."

Either way, and whichever, I say—
support your local Bitch Kitty.
Thank her for spraying the curtains of discontent,
and coughing up the hairball of inequity.

The world is her litter box because it is stinky and in need of a change.

YOU DECIDE

When to swim and when to float?
When to snub and when to dote?
When to ask the hostess for your coat?
I hate the ones who grin and gloat,
always know which way to vote
and how much baggage they should tote

Forget the choice of false or true,
turn the other cheek or sue,
and what to do in which venue—
You know your self-esteems eschew
when you can't decide on what to chew
from even a simple lunch menu

Decisive types don't understand
They wake each morning with a plan
and grab their future by the hand
They have some grit, some life command
or maybe a bigger adrenal gland
They risk the choice, commit, demand

They may swim when they should float
but at least they've left the leaky boat
and doubt doesn't have them by the throat

But there's another point of view
we hadn't covered hitherto:
"Get er done" can misconstrue!

But sweet uncertainty will countermand
the knee jerk vote and hasty stand
to save us from life's reprimand

14

I don't mean to sugarcoat
or play the sacrificial goat

My chronic lack of follow through
is way much more than déjà vu

But we ditherers may understand
the big stuff isn't in our hands

POND OF TEARS

Sitting in a county courtroom pew
Amongst the mumbling,
"That's discovery" and "Long days" hum of
clerks in cheap
and lawyers in nice
grey suits
Guarded by polite and seasoned police officers in pressed uniforms
The scales of justice
hang evenly on a laptop screen
just beyond the wood railing/riffraff divide

My son is off-stage with the other prisoners
I can see the movement of black and white stripes
through a glass square in the big metal door
A cheerful, surely stoned, out on bail, defendant
keeps buzzing around the wooden barrier asking stupid questions
The guard answers pleasantly with one hand on his gun
"Take a seat. You must take a seat."
The Judge takes attendance

I've decided to fill my koi pond with the soft tears I've cried for my children

My son's name is called
The one we proudly gave him when he was
still inside me
The name on his diplomas
It's a good name
even when you hear it in the courtroom

The bailiff's calling and charging has
the drafty indignity of a hospital gown
The crimes of the defendants are not announced over a loudspeaker
but you can make out most of the muttered charges and pleas
Their crimes and mistakes are
open at the back

I've decided to bury my expectations under my thorniest rose bush and
mulch them under with my hopes

What would we all be doing today without crack and meth
and vodka and beer?
Frisbee on the beach?
Learning to play the violin?

In the front pew a father and mother sit pillar-like on either
side of their first offender daughter
They are quietly screaming
imploding
I recognize the musty scent of dissolving dreams

The clerk at the judge's bench wonders what the kind and slightly broken
looking woman (me) is writing in her little book

She is writing to stop the feeling
She is writing to change the world

I've decided to fill my koi pond with the soft tears I've cried for all the broken
children of crack and vodka and beer

The guards begin to bring out the prisoners
who have already been here before,
like my son,
in their nicest, hoping for probation, suits
and are now wearing the striped pajamas
Their chests are all sunken with real shame or false humility
And they hold their hands behind their backs
as if in handcuffs
The one girl prisoner's striped PJs hang on her like curtains
And she has a foolish swagger the others have lost
still unaware that her gown is open at the back

I wonder why this bench is so hard to sit on, and I want to glide away and
soar over the choppy waves of the sea like a pelican and dive in and under to
the cold quiet of the deepest ocean

A girl in a nice skirt is charged with class 3 felony theft
and seems to have taken a plea
We hear "4000 dollars restitution"
It's nice to see someone stealing
maybe just to get some money and buy nice skirts
A child of greed instead of crack and meth and vodka and beer

The first offender in the front pew is called
She is joined by a lawyer with snakeskin cowboy boots
The parents slide together
She's been a part of the scheme with fancy skirt, but she gets a better deal
She's younger—led astray
She foolishly tries to whine her way through
The Judge tips his head with a frown, but Cowboy Boots saves her
Her hands are not yet behind her back
And she leaves the courtroom without
even glancing at her parents

I want to float among some big burly ocean swells and be enveloped by their cool and nearly crushing embrace

It looks as if I will sit on the hard bench again
My son's lawyer asks for a continuance
Interesting word, continuance

Before I can leave, I have to watch
as the man sitting in front of me
is called to the bench
He is wearing a Mr. Roger's Neighborhood sweater
His hands clasped in front of his belly like a priest
He is asking to be released from probation
He is no longer an angry man
He hasn't hit his son in two years
The female prosecutor doesn't like the idea
but he has a note from his wife

As I leave, the pretty lawyer with the soft pink purse with the big gold buckle
is flirting with the swarthy probation officer in the yellow tie
It is refreshing to have a little romance in amongst the restitution

I head home to bury my expectations under my thorniest rose bush, mulch them under with my hopes, and fill my koi pond with the soft tears I've cried for my children

BARE TREES

Thirteen naked pecan trees guard our winter yard
humble monuments
heroes in work clothes
poised with the graceful stillness of a frozen river,
greyer than the grey sky,
they seem to watch and ponder
some, roughly, lurk and loom
dutiful centurions
stoically, exposed and waiting

I admire their aged veteran survivor dignity
and their towering pecan wisdom:
always the last to show their leaves
and trust the spring

There is weekend in bare trees
no dropping or dripping
no industry
Their rest is our rest
too cold to
no need to
They sit quiet so
we can

Now, in December stubbornly confident
in their nude, flowing stillness
they modestly
reach for light
bend how they must
with no movement

Serenely naked, almost
willfully vulnerable

NEW LIFE SURFING

You find yourself straddling a surfboard in the
cold water of the Pacific Ocean,
the sun soaking your wet shoulders.

You are nine months pregnant, and your bloated
belly rests on the wide waxy board
like a holiday ham on a platter.

You float and water waddle out beyond the breakers,
rolling with the swells, up and down, whoosh—whoosh,
gently, hypnotically, almost relaxed.

You can just barely see the waving arms of
a small crowd on the beach; the crowd
may be cheering for you and seems to love you.

The crowd confirms and compounds your certain
and pressing need to get into shore,
while the gentle swells pull you into the deep sea.

Several businesslike surfers, tan skin and wet suits,
ride the waves in
and paddle back out.

The loud grey ocean slaps your surfboard and
pounds the shore; you call to the surfers
and a pelican carries your voice off like a tasty fish.

A quiet panic bubbles up beneath and through you
from the ocean floor; you hopelessly wave
your numb hands at the crab-sized crowd on the shore.

Sinking despair rises from the hollows
of the forming waves, and your sobs share
the rippling rhythm of the choppy sea.

Your tears swell the sea beneath your board, and the
water playfully tosses and plants you on its back
like a toddler on Daddy's shoulders.

And the swell becomes a soft, fat, rumbling
wave, a strong horse carrying you
at a gentle lope right to shore.

The crowd is your family; they are crying with joy;
you dig your toes into the sand
and go to them.

IT'S ONLY FITTING

By myself in a big fitting room at Macy's
Trying—unsuccessfully—to find a pair of jeans
I can marry and take home
really commit to
a pair of jeans that is
not necessarily classic or low rise
but has that just right Goldilocks fit
Rejecting another pair,
I say out loud:
"Who has legs this long anyway?"

And my frustration reminds me of the longing to fit
comfortably
into and with—
reminds me of my history of red-headed,
"I'll never fit in" despair
and the hunger for the snug serenity
of being the piece designed for the space

But, then, sliding the zipper and snapping the snap
on that slightly off-color pair
that turns out to hug and give and flatter like a smile
I remember fitting very well
in a small bed with my husband
on the back of a horse
in a rocking chair with a baby
in a classroom

I know the silent hum
the lock—load
and easy sliding machinery of a flush fit

The fit is not so rare
especially if I remember that
the growing and stretching
simply forward into that space
I'm *unpredictably* designed to fill
is the snug/snap fit
and struggling to fit is like
trying to shape water into a ball
instead of drinking it

LIFEGUARDING

Her fine bones, shadow sharp,
creamy skin, swollen and transparent.
Baby-hair fuzz survives around a bandana
pushed askew by pillows that seem to be swallowing her whole
Her brown eyes are ocean caves,
ache bubbling to the surface.

We lifeguards are on duty—
charming, entertaining, pretending
and like the pool bullies,
we dunk the cancer under, and
submerge ourselves in the quiet
echoing underwater peace,
bathed in cool denial
beneath the need and ravages,
the stinging, blinking glare
at the surface.

We are having tea on the pool bottom in our two-piece bathing suits.

While she,
safely in the shallows,
only moments ago,

sinks away.

PORTRAIT OF CATHY

An oil painting of my sister hung in our front door hallway
lit by morning light
scented in fall by Mom's camellias
She faced sideways,
nearly backwards
in one of our black and cane dining room chairs
She wore her childhood uniform—
a black leotard
long thin sleeves sliding off her freckled,
half-round shoulders
Her face has a splatter of freckles too and
she is wearing the Cathy look –
an enticing blend of tender and haughty

Her tan, bare legs are tightly
drawn together
as if laced to the chair leg
but fluid as falling water
Her feet, in black ballet slippers,
are poised,
maybe hungry to dance, but
her arms are lazy-folded under her chin
as if to say
I am already complicated
one part wants this
one part needs that
and my shiny as lightning hair
in the taut knot at the crown of my head
is neat as darkness
but my blue eyes
are also overcast
even at 13

Fifty years later my sister's portrait hangs on her bedroom wall
and my brother and I are watching
her live the last 4 days of her life
We are her scared and bumbling Hospice team
My older brother, Mike,
remembers the real dancing girl in the painting
following her outstretched hand
in leaps and turns across wooden floors
I was baby sister when she sat
poised and sideways in that chair,
but I recognize my big sister in the
safe, static oil and
looking over the back of her chair,
she watches cancer Cathy dissolve away beneath her

In the middle of the last long night
with muted light on dense silence
we studied and counted her breaths
and the spaces between
wanting to be a part of her last
and thinking death would come
quietly
like he does
in the movies

And, we both saw her again

We would never have known we had really seen her again
if I hadn't had to tell Mike

Resting in the twin beds of the next room
like camper's gossiping bunk to bunk, I said:
"Maybe it was just the light; I'm so damned tired, but. . .."
Mike interrupted me,
"She was young and perfect again there for a while,"
"The dancing girl," I said
We nodded,
listening closely to the whisper of joy.

NOTES ON A MEETING

Trying to find the Zen in my desk chair
while the big brains tussle and grapple
with some principles and pesky rubrics of assessment.

My chair is too low and too hard,
but I concentrate on the easy way it rolls and the back support.

Have you noticed that buzzards like to meet in dead trees?
A committee of buzzards gathers weekly in the
big dead live-oak tree on the edge of the cemetery by my house.

My chair also has a height adjustment—
I ride it up and down
and then settle in the middle and I try to care about the data,
and where it goes and
I hope someone is nourished by the data.

With just the most subtle shift of my hips
I can swivel enough to revive my soul
and I wonder how Harpo Marx landed his job.
Was he good with silence, or did he have an annoying voice?
Did he go to meetings in a trench-coat and honk his horn?
I want Harpo's job and
I'm afraid to tell the others that I am a standard deviation.

While the buzzards are meeting in their dead tree,
they dry their wings and
sniff the air for dinner
and discuss how many sides there are in an issue

They can only agree that there are more sides to an issue than a dead
armadillo.

Most importantly, the buzzards argue about what sound a clashing
paradigm makes

A snoring sound, they decide, definitively.

A dirt clod has lodged in the wheel of my chair;
without rolling, I can no longer value the back support.

When the buzzards can't stand to sit in the dead tree any longer,
they agree with the last buzzard who spoke,
and they all fly from the dead tree together.
Meeting adjourned.

FORCING SOLUTIONS

1. Stay up for late night inspection and interrogation
2. Early morning search for evidence
3. Afternoon confrontation
4. Tag team grilling
5. Write a check
6. Stand in the doorway and pry
7. Make his favorite meal
8. Search the car
9. Search the phone
10. Stand in the doorway and lecture
11. Write a check
12. Co-sign a car loan
13. Stock up on his favorite frozen pizza
14. Pay off his credit card

Repeat steps 1 through 14

15. Stand in the doorway and cry
16. Bail him out
17. Call a good lawyer
18. Write a letter to the judge
19. Call the city attorney
20. Hang up on the city attorney
21. Search his room, car and phone
22. Stand in the doorway and beg
23. Text him what you really meant to say
24. Stand in the doorway and scream
25. Throw him out
26. Stand by the car window and beg him to stay
27. Make his favorite meal

28. Pay off the credit card he got in his brother's name
29. Visit him at the county jail to lecture, beg and cry
30. Fight with your husband
31. Visit him at the county jail to lecture, beg and cry

Repeat steps 1–31 as many times as you must

WAVE RIDE

Quickly kicking, bubble blowing, plow the sand and push
Softly split the slippery surface, to greet the welcome sun
And meet the sparkling pause between the swell and rush

Swollen swells, sexy rolling riding round and lush
Carried, swallowed, chased and chasing come
Quickly kicking, bubble blowing, plow the sand and push

Shoulder deep, floating dance inside the water's hush
Cool and curling water shadows jump and hum
And join the sparkling pause between the swell and rush

Float cold and wet within the plunging, deep and plush
Ready, brave and frightened diving through beyond
Quickly kicking, bubble blowing, plow the sand and push

Taken, rolled, stolen, lost amidst the crush
and grainy mush; taken tumbled tossed and spun
to lose the sparkling pause between the swell and rush

Escape the sandy frothy swirling slush
Toppled, swept and flailing, tourists turn and run
Quickly kicking, bubble blowing, plow the sand and push
And find the sparkling pause between the swell and rush

LOST THINGS

This weekend I hunted for lost things, specifically,
I hunted for the only thing
I wanted and took with me when my parents' life
got packed and sorted and moved to Assisted Living:
The ceramic nativity set of my childhood, the one
my father and I set up each Christmas in the den bookshelves
complete with angels in angel's hair, a camel for the kings
and a barn for baby Jesus

I moved the tradition to my own living room bookshelf,
packed it carefully away after that first Christmas
and haven't seen it since

My daughter used to find my lost things
sometimes because she had lost them
sometimes because
she was young and didn't yet have her own things to lose

My Dad, ninetyish, loses things everyday
mostly small things, keys and nail clippers and
sometimes another of his breakfast friends from the building
The last time I visited, he thought he'd lost
his favorite *Member's Only* jacket
the tan one
and he woke fretting and searching his mind
and then the apartment

He'd lent the coat to me the day before,
so, we found it on my back
Dad was greatly relieved,
then embarrassed,
and then, he lost his pen

In the great big middle of life,
you accept the loss of certain things:
energy, hair, some muscle tone,
and you embrace the loss of others:
emotional intensity, all-nighters, childbirth.
You're grateful you haven't lost
some of the more vital things: no organs yet—
not even tonsils or gallbladder—just a bit of knee meniscus,
and a snip of finger to a Cuisinart

If you think about it, you're damn surprised
by some of the things you haven't yet lost:
your parents
that denim work shirt from high school
your daughter's first tennis shoes
your sense of humor

And there are the things you have hopefully just misplaced:
your son
your childhood friend
your libido
your faith in humanity

You can also be thankful for the collateral benefits
of your search for lost things:
closet cleaning
garage reorganization
that buoyant anticipation as you search and
imagine finding the thing
and never searching again.

And we must be thankful, finally, for the things we have found—
without or after we've given up looking:
that 20-dollar bill in a coat pocket
a new friend
an earring on the garage floor,
your faith in God

DADDY'S POSTCARDS (IN MEMORY OF MY FATHER)

I love this one
It is probably my favorite
The picture is a little red-haired girl
perched but cozy on her Daddy's lap
She is 5 or 6
missing some teeth
swarm of freckles
He is watching her with kind green eyes
His long arms,
joined by the book of art prints he holds in her lap,
encircle and wrap her up
They are studying Renoir again
her favorite, of course,
because of all those redheads
Beautiful
"Like you," the Daddy says to her,
cupping her head under his chin

The message on the back reads:
You'll never forget this
guiding love
this calm or
this joyful connection with beauty
captured in paint and in your memory
—-50 years later
You'll sit in a Paris museum and
still in my lap
you'll enter this painting
with the little red-haired girl in the blue dress
and with me
We'll see her again, together

This next postcard had a hard time finding me
I was so hard to find that *I* didn't know where I was
It pictures a young writer
Probably unknown
She is at work at a desk, in a bed, on a plane, in a campsite

The message on the back reads:
Like me,
This is the way you'll work things out
I know how you feel
Make a plan
Live a routine
Keep writing

This card is from Broadway
Behind the marquis you can see guys and dolls and
strippers and wildebeests,
the sharks and the jets,
phantoms and cats and cowboys and
rainmakers and old maids and they bring in the clowns
You can hear the voices
of everyone you've
met and know
and will never know
gathered,
and you can feel
The audience savoring the tasty tones
thick—creamy—delicious
perfectly nourishing, so filling so
satisfying
You have to smile and cry

The message on the back reads:
We saw a great show last night. . .
We almost didn't go because we were pooped—
done
worn out with fighting the misbehaving world—
but then we saw what we can do
to show and tell each other and
the hope that's alive in
these careful knots tied between us
And so now,
armored with artistry,
we are smiling and crying again and
humming that haunting tune

Each postcard in this pile was sent to one of the grandkids
Castles and otters and basilicas and
children just like them from another hemisphere
great paintings
great dancers
great buildings
great memories

The message on the back reads:
Do what you love
Bend the boundaries
Pack your fears
Unpack your dreams

I got this last postcard just the other day
Words will never really do the picture justice
Blue-orange skies—shooting stars—honeysuckle— waves breaking

The message on the back reads:
Arrived safely
Hope you are well
Miss you, but we are having a grand time
See you when we see you,
Love, always,
Daddy

EVERY NINTH WAVE

These are the rules:

Stay shoulder deep in the cold Pacific Ocean, the crisp sun on your wet head.
(You can use another ocean, but the Pacific is best, so heavy and strong and
deliberate)

Face the waves,
Never stand or run,
Wait for a thick, round wave, like a sexy woman.
(It takes some time to recognize these, but that is the game.)

Ride the wave as far as it will take you.
A good wave will lift and embrace you and carry you to the shallows.
Don't stay in the sandy whitewater:
paddle back out,
dig your fingers into the sand and pull,
kick and swim.
Never stand up!

Of course, the waves keep coming,
you have to pull and kick like hell
or the next wave will grab and
roll and grind you.
If you are quick,
if you are ready,
brave and focused,
you make it on time—
better yet,
you are just in time.

You dive through;
you take the wave,
chased and chasing,
cool and curling over your back.
Your friends have taken the wave too,
laughing on the other side,
in the valley between.

Some things to remember:
Children are better at this game, and
there is the ninth wave.

Was it my so tan big sister
(in her waist high, dotted-Swiss two-piece bathing suit)
repeating the wisdom of the smooth, shimmering
Lifeguards up on their orange stands?
Or my father, also tan,
everyone tan but me.
I'm forever freckled.

It was probably Daddy who warned us:
"Never turn your back on the waves!"

The tourists toppled like toddlers.

But the ninth wave was surfer myth.
The sets would tumble in,
and you could take wave one and four and seven for granted.
But the ninth wave had the scope to crush you.
If you're shoulder deep in the game,
you simply must swim to it,
or the swirling, sandy white-water machine will guzzle you.

Kick hard, and dive under and through it.

Close your eyes, and be swallowed;

accepted;

devoured as a piece of the quiet humming underneath world.

Arrive breathless,

in the deep sparkling pause on the other side.

Float, shoulder deep—

The sun on your wet hair.

MOST OF ALL (IN MEMORY OF MY MOTHER)

Most of all, you were cool,
smooth palms on my fever

You are driving me
many afternoons a week
in that tiny yellow bubble of a car
The one they quit making
A mother-daughter time capsule
Puttering the slow lane
of the after-school Santa Ana freeway
Other cars in fast motion
We are sluggishly navigating our hard transitions
Mine is more obvious than yours—I am 13
We talk—we are silent—we are content
in the temporary
grace of our certain fulfillment of each other's needs
We stop for El Rancho enchiladas before
returning to the empty house
shaded in dusk

Most of all, you were cool,
smooth palms on my fever

When the earth shook—for real
the big quake, before dawn, senior year
life flying off the shelves
and all times otherwise
I called out
You talked me to the doorway

Most of all, you were cool,
smooth palms on my fever

I know it was hard being so strong
like those exquisitely enduring trees
along the coast you loved
Rooted in rock
pushed, shoved, caressed, bent
staying the tides and winds with
nearly broken evergreen spirit

Most of all, you were cool,
smooth palms on my fever

I hear you warning me,
frustrated by your own wisdom,
"There are no absolutes, Sal."
You weren't often wrong,
but those of us who knew your love,
knew it was absolute.

Most of all, you were cool,
smooth palms on my fever

LET'S MAKE A DEAL

If I slap your mouth
clean
off your face, will you stop?
The face God made inside me
The face I bathed in the kitchen sink
The face I kissed for fever

If I slap your mouth
clean
off your face, will you stop?
The first mouth to feed at my breast
The mouth that has smiled up and over
and then down at me in every season,
on every day until becoming
The mouth that forms the lies
The mouth that twists in shame

If I cry enough, a pond. . .a lake. . ..an ocean,
will you stop?
Tears like those you cried for my milk
like those you have cried for yourself
and have somehow forgotten
If I cry enough, will you stop?

If I make myself so sick because of you,
will you stop?
Sick as you were with scarlet fever
when you asked me,
your young eyes bloodshot with fear,
"What will become of me?"
Sick as you are each time you stop?

If I pray, enough will You stop him?

If I stop trying to stop you,
will you stop?

In time for me to see?
In time?

The River Never Worries

FLYING HUSBAND

My husband has taken flight

He still comes home,
but he has returned to the air,
which maybe I should worry about
or take part in
But, best to let him
have back this air
sparrow hawk freedom
we took from him

He would say given
He would say—worth it
Love rich and grounding
sloppy with earthy goodness
wallowing even in the deep muddy responsibility
the sucking clay of all we wanted to give them
and all we took and shared
Happily mired in the love muck of family

But then,
after a good long time and
before we knew it
we were anchored in the burden bog
buried by controlling forces beyond invisible
and we bubbled under
lost sight of the air
settled underground
and adapted like moles
growing what claws we needed
to dig through and upholster the mushy sludge

And now, my husband,
who has always hated caves
was the first to look up
And he has taken to the air again

I smile up at him
He wags his wings
and my feet are beginning to leave the ground
with a lighter step

POETS AND ANTIDEPRESSANTS

My good friend tells me, "You don't have to suffer."
Really?
As a conditionally sad person
not tempted to put her head in the oven,
I should stay up and write it down.
Right?
Lose sleep
after the dog has quit watching
and
sit in the garden
pencil the pain
revise the resentments
under the solar lanterns glowing jade and lapis
between me and the amber stars

When I swallow the pills, I don't notice
I sleep through the hot August night full of metaphors

And I even forget the big easy times when life was a puff of hope
a staircase of footy pajamas

If I take the yellow pills, maybe
I'll write about the cooing of doves
and the constancy of stars

But, I'll dodge the razor wire poems
bright even circles
sharp enough to cut the feet off
poor
unsuspecting pigeons

KNITTING LESSONS

I have learned to knit
as old fabric unravels
keeping an even tension
beside the pulse of emotions
working a steady pattern
fervently focused in still

My mother was puzzled, still
judging my doings, to knit
was cud chewing— a pattern
for (k)nit-wits, afraid and unraveled
by the delicious mess of emotions
life's yummy electricity of tension

Colors folding together, the tension
of stitches, purling and slipping, still
complimentary and dependent like emotions
the yarns follow, obey and knit
into a sock or a hat, combating what unravels
and resists humble patterns

My mother's daughter, for me, patterns
smelled of death and I savored tension
especially when *I* pulled the string to unravel
the daily, quiet, sameness, still
in the days when close knit
meant a family thread of routine emotions

And then, the days when I believed in emotions
as truth, as solvable puzzles, as a pattern
to follow and understand and knit
together or pull apart or talk the tension
to death, as if resolved and still,
until the next same feelings unravel

Now, I let BIG hands handle the unravel
and Fridays, we Stitch Bitches purl the week's emotions
around one of our coffee tables, listening still
and concerned; ripping out slips in our patterns
or raucously needle jousting the tension
into surrender; we band of knitters, tightly knit

In the midst of knit, my worries, like my yarn, unravel
with warm and steady tension, pulling even my emotions
inside the quietly comforting pattern so deep within still.

SON AT REST

"Cause of Death: (your) Enlarged Heart"
the first heart to beat beside my own,
so huge, so complete and tender
from the start—so wide and kind.
In pictures you peek at us from another, brighter place
"His face is like porcelain" Nana said, perfectly fragile.

What saturating joy you brought—not fragile
or fleeting, but robust like the Alps, the Pacific, like the heart
of God, and we guzzled you, and our place
in the world was as new as you. Our very own
future lived in every movement, every smile, every kind
glint inside your ancient infant eyes, so wise and impossibly tender

We were born from you, Son, and your tender
strength and perfection made our fears fragile
and nourished our hopes with a kind
of blind courage and hunger for living. The heart
we borrowed from you and forever own
in, at least, our memories, is always, still, a safe, spacious place

I choose to remember the boy who had and knew a place
to be only himself: a kitchen table, a bed, a tender
brother to be rough with, owning his own
fortress of family, where only pretense was fragile,
built atop a deep cellar of love, a catacomb heart
where moments of us are kept, stored, true and kind.

I choose or maybe know to picture you in a kind
of glowing fog, so clearly like the place
along the creek, amongst the cedars, your heart
beating inside me, when we were in a storm of tender
black and orange, a breeze of Monarchs, fragile
hoards, fluttering eyelashes, making every needle their own.

This may sound like I'm okay and don't want to own
you again or make you over in fast forward and feel your kind
long arms around me; like I'm not frozen, frightened and fragile,
or like there will ever be a time when the place
I am standing doesn't want you next to me. No. But the tender
spots of loss do retreat to the safe room you built in my heart.

Grief is a pleading heart, missing yours so truer than my own—
too large and tender and kind to stay.
You are soft light back in your brighter place—safely, perfectly fragile.

PUPPY LOVE

O Silliest of Sillies, Oh Monty my Moo
you trim up my tatters and soothe my distraught
you're my lamb-flavored cookie, my beef-basted chew

You blurry my worry and bury my blues
with your wag and your swagger, your tippy toe trot
O Silliest of Sillies, Oh Monty my Moo

Eyes fretfully bugged bark devotion so true
ears brightly akimbo, lovely tummy of spots
you're my lamb-flavored cookie, my beef-basted chew

My chicken scrap! My squeaky toy! You settle my stews
you nuzzle serene my mind fraught with thought
O Silliest of Sillies, Oh Monty my Moo

My closet in thunder, my disposition guru
you iron my wrinkles; you quell overwrought
you're my lamb-flavored cookie, my beef-basted chew

In grief, in bleak, in bummer, in glummer, your- "Woo Woo"
my Moo Moo, unravels my tangled emotional knots
O Silliest of Sillies, Oh Monty my Moo
you're my lamb-flavored cookie, my beef-basted chew

JUST

Just get over it and follow directions
while you split some atoms with a paint brush.
Just let go of that and write him off,
then build a cornflower out of your grief.
Just close your eyes and go to sleep
and toggle-nut Part A to D to form a circle

Just learn to trust the circle
and cycles and just change any direction
that steeps your sleep
in trolls with tolls. Just brush
the tangles from your grief
and tell your fears to fuck right off.

Just move on— just go with the flow right off
the planet. Just quit the gravity and circle
the moon in your ball-cap rocket, sipping grief
from your slipper. Just find your very own special direction
while you grow a peach in your hair and brush
up on astrophysics in your sleep.

Just tell me what you're feeling and sleep
through the turbulence. Just wipe that look right off
your face and make a butterfly out of a brush
pile. Please, just finish up—before you circle
the possibilities and just forget the careful direction
and directions that have caused you such grief.

Just be yourself and then sail your pond of grief
to the Big Apple and feast and sleep.
Just believe in people: ask Asian tourists for directions
on the subway. Just OPEN UP! Where do you get off
double bow-knotting the un-broken circle
and sweeping up your worries with a toothbrush?

The tool, you Tool, is to push broom that scary brush
with flying monkeys into the green sea. Wash that grief
in some baking soda and cider vinegar, and circle
your bed with silk memories soaked in sleep.
Just remember or just forget to jump off
your curvy just crazy uncharted direction

If just is a just (righteous) direction, the adverbial jab to briskly brush
grimy inertia just right off your stubborn, recyclable, dread and grief,
then just let the anxiety monster sleep and just dive into the circle.

A YEAR LATER

I see the four of you floating together
entwined vapors like vines in bloom
fragrant with love and certainty
your chatter and laughter humming
like bees in honeysuckle and joy in memories
and the time is always summer twilight

Down here the crying is regular as twilight,
but Ache and Disbelief aren't together
anymore. Ache works with Lost Memories,
and Disbelief works alone. His delusions bloom
early like morning glories, winking and humming
an impossibly catchy tune with cruel certainty

I imagine you may be bored with the certainty,
but now you know how they serve up twilight.
Are you watching or knowing or just humming
cowboy tunes and riding clouds together?
If you've got some pull, make my roses bloom
and run a refresh on my, our, memories

I've been busy weeding the memories
and regrets, hoping you left with certainty—
even though. That googly-eyed cactus did bloom
the week you died, and in the hot July twilight,
we huddled stunned-crushed-frozen together
while life so strangely-rudely kept on humming

I hope it was you stroking my feet, a tender humming
fog that morning? I have glowing memories
of you inside, before you were born, when together
our side by side souls knew each other with Holy certainty;
you were that brightest light floating like Venus at twilight,
so, I know it was you, surprising me, like a winter bloom

If it was you that made the cactus bloom
then let me hear your new voice humming
like lightning, or make tomorrow's twilight
blue, or send me some dream memories
only we would know and give me some certainty
that you are there and safe and all together

Kind spirit of memories rest your hands with certainty
on my shoulders and together we will sip hope's
bloom like hummingbirds swimming in twilight.

DEFINITIONS

Grief is a windy night
and a still morning
a restless void
a clingy companion
who needs nothing from you

Sorrow is greedy gravity
and heavy as water
to float on
to swim through
who gently drowns with you

Loss is a cozy room
and a forgotten joy
made of glass or
darkness or expectation
who follows like shadows

Faith is a neglected garden
and quiet as air
hiding like a child
too close to see
who feels lonely as God

Hope is a buried fossil
and a thorny rose bush
longing for rain
to bloom again
who is really not to blame

Joy is an infant
either way
tender and present
as light as sound
who only wants to be found

LEAKY POND

The fishpond's chronic leak
puts you in the business of digging
through mud and scorpions, forever
working to find and repair
so (your world as) the water will
stay, fixed, constant and level.

The pond leak, and its fidelity, levels
you. A friendly distraction from the life leaks,
maybe hemorrhages, you know will
need tender and tactical digging,
costly tools and professional repair,
or, more likely, will dribble on forever.

You could let this leak, leak on forever.
Use the well to keep the water level—
forget the draught and dreams of repair.
Some plants nearby are loving the leak;
they are tired of you stomping and digging,
callously, obsessively doing what you will.

Roses blooming on your leak-denial will
struggle with a fix and even fade forever,
but the Desert Willow is so-not digging
the soggy, squishy, boggy level
of moist, dropping its blooms, leaking
its green finger leaves in protest for the repair.

And you need this quest and acts of repair,
simple as hot sand. You know the chase will
fill your sleepless nights, tracking the only leak
you have any real chance of fixing forever.
So, you get help with heavy lifting and level
the rocks until you can put to rest all digging.

You simplify and rebuild, only digging
up the patience to slowly and truly repair
what's broken and quietly shape and level
and double check, so this one leak will
be a story you tell for a time, remember forever—
this distraction fix tourniquet for unfixable leaks

Watching the water flow sure and level, the soothing agony of digging done,
your faithful friend, the leak, finally beyond patched to repaired, and
your will rejuvenated by one simple thing mended (maybe) forever.

THE UPGRADE

Long way
Texas to London and back
and you know the details coming back
cramped-swollen-hungry-sleepy
rudely swarming
lines, lines, lines

Then the upgrade
You deserve it
You need it
Two years of lost and carried baggage
Sequestered
Quarantined
like the grief was infectious
the loss contagious

And yet the upgrade was really
unearned
"How did this happen?"
Your surprise speaks
holding up the new ticket

She raises an eyebrow to compliment her
flight attendant wisdom:
"Some things you must never question"

Needed
Undeserved
Luxury
Deliciously comfy
Scrumptiously free
Our paying cabin mates
could never taste the pleasure like
the imposters in 4 C&D

Serenely swallowed by the huge
tenderly adjustable seats
Each perk-
appetizers
fine wines
little overnight bags
sleep masks and fuzzy sock slippers
spreading a new layer of pleasure
like cold feet in warm sand
Each round of service a soul massage
like only God could arrange this for us

Was there proof of God in the upgrade?
A hug, then a pat, a reassuring squeeze
a stroke against doubt
carried on the hum
caressed by the vibration
cuddled close inside the vacuum
Gliding
Reclining into certainty
goodness
love
We fly

CHANGE RING

A Change Ring works just like this poem, with sounds
for words and notes for feelings. The deep,
discordant pairs beat and pull and build
restless suspense for notes we love to ring
again, or the surprising neighbors to join once more,
before the consoling and tidy scale returns

*Like waiting for the kiss, afraid the kiss will change everything, until you
enter the moment and let the kiss bend time forever*

Cross and Switch—Cross and Switch

The notes are time, sometimes longing to return
rewind, replay, (no faint echoes), only sounds
at volume, crisp colors, tasty, true and more
than easy, full, pulsing, sweeping, deep
moments shared around a table, a ring
of tomorrows we knew we could build

*Like the baby's head under her rib, inside the whoosh, beside their hearts.
Then his cry breaking the air with joy.*

Cross and Switch—Cross and Switch

The notes are love that doesn't see itself build
or burn or roll along or notice the return,
steady as air. The neat and always rumbling ring,
whale songs drowning vibrato beneath the sound
and surface, warm waves and currents, echoing deep,
certain, satisfied with this and now and no more.

*Like her waist melting under the touch of his hand
And decades later, their fingers welding together before his surgery*

Cross and Switch—Cross and Switch

The notes are change, dreaded, welcome, more
hoped for than fought for; change that builds
pianissimo, assured, unnoticed, or strikes forte deep:
CRESCENDOS, twisting, shaking, demanding no return,
obliterating even regret, a reverberating sound
that closes the old and begins the new ring

> *Like playing in the waves with your dad while your mother worries on the shore,*
> *Then worrying on the shore while your husband plays in the waves with your son.*

Cross and Switch—Cross and Switch

In the silence between rounds, the damped, stop-ring
caesura, the deep breath, aching with much more
or too little time, longing for the fresh sound,
deserving the kind, soft chance to build
or hold, fermata, to hide and never return
and linger in between in silence soft and deep

> *Like the clinging need of a feverish child*
> *And the casually confident wave and nod when they smile and leave.*

Cross and Switch—Cross and Switch

We may think we want to stay in the deep
before or after— inside and between the ring
halt-pulse, hold-breathe, stop-beat, no return
never wake with heart pounding surprise or more
of the same-same—never muster, gather, begin, rebuild,
expect, console, listen, wait, worry, or long for another sound

Like the dark dawn of fresh grief
And the someday grace of a perfect moment remembered

Cross and Switch—Cross and Switch

But sounds soft as dawn build and
nudge us one more time, in time, every time,
another deep need rings out our return.

STILL BEGINNING

Dear Parents of Dead Children,
I need to talk to you and only you and
never tell the others about the
shadowy weight of
Still

Still on replay,
like that wren's tedious song
just as I'm waking

You. Alone. Dying.

Still
staring out windows
for signs and visions
wondering. . .if I'd only. . .
struggling to form your face
missing for you what you are missing,
mining for proof you are finally fine,

I
stood in the doorway
sat in my car
prayed like a prisoner
hoped like a child

Whenever we see a Great Blue Heron
so long and gracefully gawky
we think it is you
I test God
if I see a heron this morning, he's with You
Sometimes God passes

A tall lost soul on an old bicycle
peddling the highway this morning
bear on a tricycle
I slow down; it might be you; it was all a mistake
three years later
my cruel trick mind
Still
teasing me

I
stood in the doorway
sat in my car
prayed like a prisoner
hoped like a child

Still longing to dream of you
but you're off camera
living underground with Nana
who hadn't thought to tell me
you were still alive.

I catch a glimpse of you
your walk,
the swing of your wide shoulders,
but your face is
fuzzy freezer mist
between
gone and becoming
with some quiet promise
of beginning

Like beginning to speak of you
in past tense without pausing
Accept the "Oh" in front of your name
Oh, Ian. . .. . .
Trust I was powerless
Savor and soak deeply in the missing of you
Feel you here for the good times

Even though I
stood in the doorway
sat in my car
prayed like a prisoner
hoped like a child

FOUR YEARS GONE AND HERE

You are four years gone now, and I'm thinking
about the time when you were four years here.
Little brother arrived early and had to stay
in the hospital. You had to scrub your hands
and wear a yellow paper gown to see.
You touched his head and adored him instantly.

We were yours, complete surrender, but instantly,
he was your only wish fulfilled and you are thinking
about what brothers do, brown eyes somehow seeing,
into the backyard future when your bigger hand
would hold his hand and lead him playfully from here
to anywhere with tenderness so true it stays

Every minute about him. Nana came to stay.
We didn't know to know, but she knew instantly—
the difference. No rivalry. You wanted him here
at home: an angel's love born before thinking—
just as if a floating piece of you was now in your hand.
You caught it, held it gently and wanted everyone to see.

Brown Roper boots—red terry hoody—longing to see
you more clearly—lasso live snapshots that stay
and never leave—your smell—the feel of your hand.
Your cheek meets your pony's muzzle and instantly
all big eyes soften—sawdust and alfalfa. Thinking
of all the wasted seconds I forgot you were here.

I may do this every year you're not here:
try to remember your fifth year next and see
if I can conjure connections and crush thinking
about missed-missing-lost-strayed—to stay
close to that soft soul I know and not instantly
default to the loss, the stolen—my empty hand.

Maybe now, at least in a poem, I feel your hand
taking mine—long light fingers— just here
for a little while. I sigh, knowing the touch instantly,
trying not to clutch at it and crush it. Eyes closed, I see
you now—healed, and your face content and meant to stay
where you are found—beyond love and all thinking.

At first thinking was unthinkable, swallowed in feeling with only
secondhand joys. But nothing stays or lasts here—Oh no! —and Thank God.
We still see, too instantly, the empty chair, but now you are
sometimes, somehow, sitting there.

SAVING A SEAT

Son,
We hadn't seen you
as the Great Blue Heron
in too long

Between holidays
Stress morphing to grief
We walked our walk
beside the sleepy winter pasture
down to the river

I said, "I need a heron today."
We turned the bend of the road together

Crossing the new bridge that's only seen one flood,
Dad said, "There he is."

Hunched in the damp chill
on a crooked limb
of the biggest dead Cypress
there you were
still and stoic and staying
saving a seat
the flood renewed river
running young below you

Not the usual fly-over-wing-wag

You let us walk the whole bridge
there and back

I made us turn back a bit early,
before the trees on the bank
to keep my eye on you
and watch you fly away if you needed to

But you stayed

No hunting today
You were there to say
I am (still) here.

YOUR YOGA TEACHER REMINDS YOU THAT JOY IS FOREVER (*THANK YOU STEPHANIE SNYDER*)

A bird may shit on your shoulder the day after your son dies,
but in some countries, this is considered lucky.
Your car may break down that same day and you may lock
yourself out of your house. You think the universe doesn't care
about your son. You are right. It can't care or make or own
your best or worst memories or remind you—that joy is for forever.

But porch wrens will build nests in his big shoes, for me, forever.
The gentle tilt of his head and infant god-like smile never dies.
My young son, wrapping himself around his good dog—this snap I own.
His long fingers folded around a basketball; a trillion lucky
moments I forgot to collect are stored inside the way he cared
even from behind and around too many bars with so many locks.

On the anniversary of that cruel day, when I have locked
myself inside my fortress of regret with supplies to last forever,
my grandchild may run to me and throw her arms, with careless
abandon, around my knees. Like a wave that breaks and dies
peacefully on its firm and thirsty shore, my pain melts. So lucky,
I think, and I begin to see all the smiles and moments I still own.

The ache for him does sit like a fat black dog on my chest. We own
each other until kindness or gratitude work the rusty lock
of our kennel. Or a heron flies over, just then, and I nod, so lucky
to have everything but him. Too many years the grief was for forever
But here's the good news for, just, everyone: the pain can die
A very slow death, reborn as best memories, in your tender care.

And, deep pain also triggers the big reveal on exactly who cares
enough or just knows not to fix it and allows you to own
that your loss is not a "journey" that becomes a less-loss or dies.
Your loss may be the enemy you befriend, hold close and keep locked
in your regret-room-should-have-forgot-to hope chest almost forever,
until one morning *you* decide to no longer label disaster as "just my luck"

Then grief, the uncomfortable chair, sits in the corner alone and unlucky,
And you are not tempted to sit for long. Like deadwood carefully
pruned from a rose, time and love snip away at the frightful forever—
week by day by hour by moment you swap the sorrow you once owned
because we know, don't we, just as the robin knows spring, that all locks
are ours to work when we are ready and are reminded that joy never dies.

Grace, not luck, lent me that perfect first-born love. I still own the weight
of him on my lap and feel his caring hand on my shoulder whenever I let
faith armlock fear and remember joy is forever and love never dies.